1-1

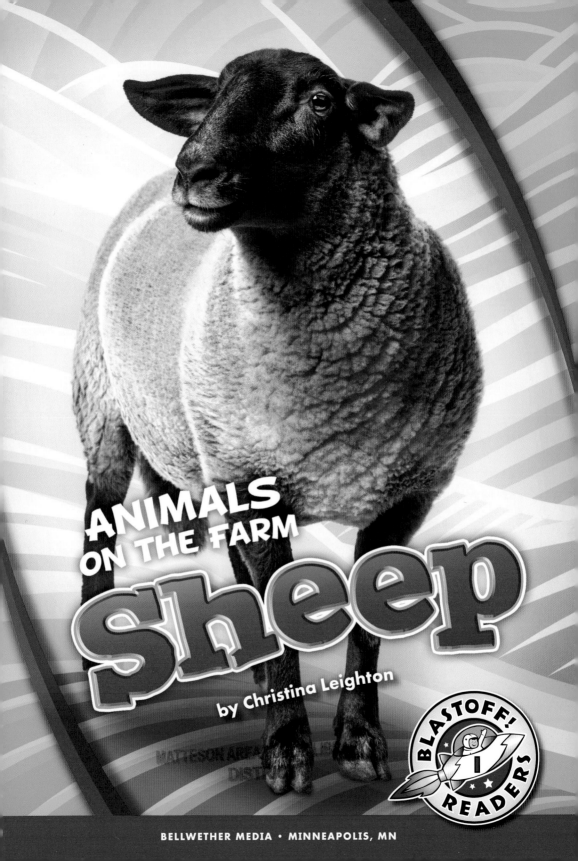

ANIMALS ON THE FARM

Sheep

by Christina Leighton

BELLWETHER MEDIA • MINNEAPOLIS, MN

Note to Librarians, Teachers, and Parents:

Blastoff! Readers are carefully developed by literacy experts and combine standards-based content with developmentally appropriate text.

Level 1 provides the most support through repetition of high-frequency words, light text, predictable sentence patterns, and strong visual support.

Level 2 offers early readers a bit more challenge through varied simple sentences, increased text load, and less repetition of high-frequency words.

Level 3 advances early-fluent readers toward fluency through increased text and concept load, less reliance on visuals, longer sentences, and more literary language.

Level 4 builds reading stamina by providing more text per page, increased use of punctuation, greater variation in sentence patterns, and increasingly challenging vocabulary.

Level 5 encourages children to move from "learning to read" to "reading to learn" by providing even more text, varied writing styles, and less familiar topics.

Whichever book is right for your reader, Blastoff! Readers are the perfect books to build confidence and encourage a love of reading that will last a lifetime!

This edition first published in 2018 by Bellwether Media, Inc.

No part of this publication may be reproduced in whole or in part without written permission of the publisher. For information regarding permission, write to Bellwether Media, Inc., Attention: Permissions Department, 5357 Penn Avenue South, Minneapolis, MN 55419.

Library of Congress Cataloging-in-Publication Data

Names: Leighton, Christina, author.
Title: Sheep / by Christina Leighton.
Description: Minneapolis, MN : Bellwether Media, Inc., [2018] | Series:
    Blastoff! Readers. Animals on the Farm | Audience: Ages 5-8. | Audience: K
    to Grade 3. | Includes bibliographical references and index.
Identifiers: LCCN 2017029539 | ISBN 9781626177260 (hardcover : alk. paper) |
    ISBN 9781681035062 (ebook)
Subjects: LCSH: Sheep–Juvenile literature.
Classification: LCC QL737.U53 L444 2018 | DDC 636.3-dc23
LC record available at https://lccn.loc.gov/2017029539

Editor: Rebecca Sabelko   Designer: Lois Stanfield

Printed in the United States of America, North Mankato, MN.

Table of Contents

Time for a Haircut!

Sheep rest in the shade. Their fluffy **wool** makes them too hot.

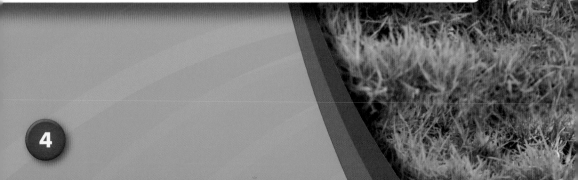

A farmer **shears** their wool. Now the sheep are ready for summer!

What Are Sheep?

Sheep are **mammals** with four legs and **split hooves**.

split
hoof

Most sheep have
thick, white wool.
It can also be
black or brown.

Wool is sheared
every spring.
It can be used to
make clothes.

sheep
wool

sheared
sheep

Some male sheep have big, curled horns. Female sheep may have small horns.

curled
horns

male sheep

Life on the Farm

Sheep stick together in **flocks**. They spend time in **pastures** and barns.

NAMES:

males:	rams
females:	ewes
babies:	lambs

flock

The flock eats grass
and other plants.
They may eat hay
in the barn.

FAVORITE FOODS:

grass and hay

The farmer gets wool and milk from his sheep. Time to tend to his flock!

Glossary

flocks

groups of sheep

shears

cuts wool

mammals

warm-blooded animals that have hair and feed their young milk

split hooves

hard foot coverings that are divided into two parts

pastures

large fields where sheep can feed on grasses

wool

the soft, thick hair of sheep

To Learn More

AT THE LIBRARY

Arnold, Quinn M. *Sheep*. Mankato, Minn.: Creative Education and Creative Paperbacks, 2017.

Hasselius, Michelle. *Sheep*. North Mankato, Minn.: Capstone Press, 2017.

Leaf, Christina. *Baby Sheep*. Minneapolis, Minn.: Bellwether Media, 2014.

ON THE WEB

Learning more about sheep is as easy as 1, 2, 3.

1. Go to www.factsurfer.com.

2. Enter "sheep" into the search box.

3. Click the "Surf" button and you will see a list of related web sites.

With factsurfer.com, finding more information is just a click away.

Index

The images in this book are reproduced through the courtesy of: Eric Isselee, front cover; DavidYoung, pp. 4-5; Berna Namoglu, pp. 6-7; BackyardProduction, pp. 8-9; fotomarekka, pp. 10-11; Sponner, pp. 12-13; francesco de marco, p. 13; Zbyszko, pp. 14-15; smereka, pp. 16-17; Duncan Andison, pp. 18-19; Estudi Vaque, pp. 20-21; Mimadeo, p. 22 (top left); PatrikStedrak, p. 22 (middle left); Dashu Xinganling, p. 22 (bottom left); Mats, p. 22 (top right); NEO80, p. 22 (middle right); Anna Hoychuk, p. 22 (bottom right).